WHAT THE ARTIST SAW

Claude Monet

*He saw the world
in a brilliant light*

Written by
Amy Guglielmo

Illustrated by
Ginnie Hsu

On November 14, 1840, on the fifth floor of
a small apartment building, near the Seine River in
Paris, Oscar-Claude Monet was born. We know him
today as Claude Monet. Claude lived with his older
brother and parents. His father worked as a grocer,
but his business was failing, and they didn't
have much money.

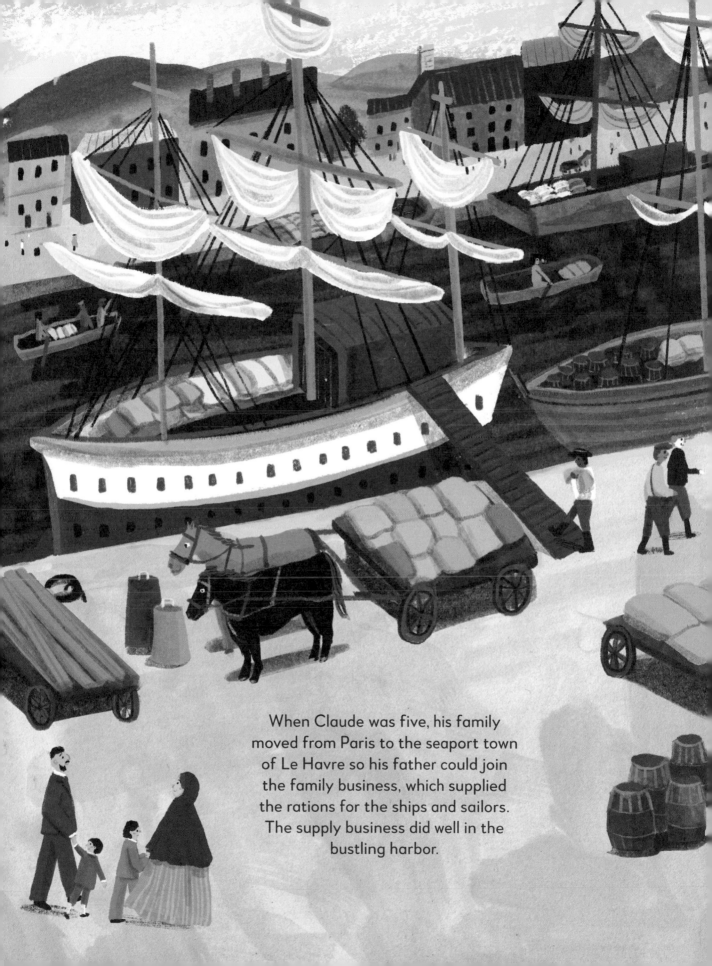

When Claude was five, his family moved from Paris to the seaport town of Le Havre so his father could join the family business, which supplied the rations for the ships and sailors. The supply business did well in the bustling harbor.

At school, Claude learned reading, writing, mathematics, and spelling, but he didn't enjoy school. Instead of doing his classwork, he spent much of the school day doodling funny pictures of his teachers in his books.

On many days, he skipped school entirely to be outside in the fields, wandering on the dunes by the sea. He already knew he wanted to become an artist. His mother encouraged his first drawings.

Sit and *watch the world go by.*

Try drawing or painting the people you see.

At age 15, Claude started drawing cartoonish
pictures of local people. His drawings achieved
notoriety and people commissioned his portraits.
Because he had learned about business from his
family's store, he managed to sell his drawings
and save up some money.

But then his mother died just after he turned 16. It was around this time that Claude left school. His aunt Marie-Jeanne helped raise him, and recognizing his talent, she encouraged art lessons. He still enjoyed drawing caricatures and sold his drawings in a local shop.

Then, he met artist Eugène Boudin. Boudin was known for his dreamy coastal paintings. He encouraged Claude to paint outdoors!

The invention of portable paint tubes allowed artists to take their paints outside. Boudin took Claude along to paint with him in nature and introduced him to a new technique called painting *en plein air* (in open air). He showed young Claude how light played and danced on the surface of the water.

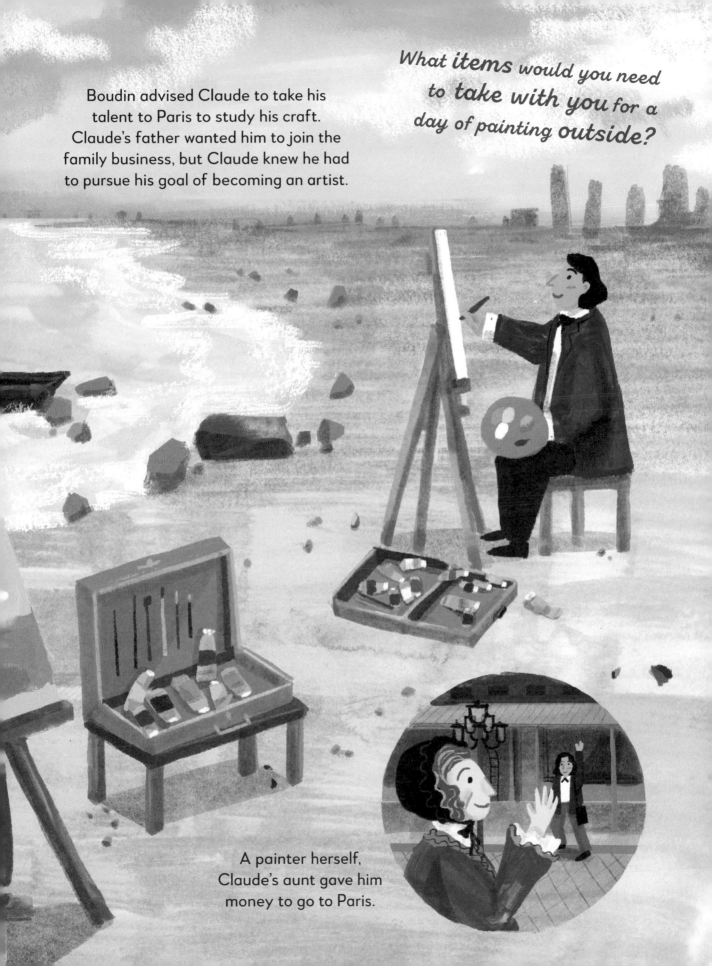

Boudin advised Claude to take his talent to Paris to study his craft. Claude's father wanted him to join the family business, but Claude knew he had to pursue his goal of becoming an artist.

What items would you need to take with you for a day of painting outside?

A painter herself, Claude's aunt gave him money to go to Paris.

Claude eagerly moved to Paris to study painting at the Académie Suisse. This was more of a studio than a "proper" school, since there were no lessons or exams.

Do you think it is **easy** or difficult to draw **people** realistically?

There, he learned to paint live models, but he didn't enjoy the old-fashioned way of painting. And he really didn't like painting indoors.

Still, he made friends with some other young artists, visited galleries, and toured working artists' studios. He enjoyed meeting up with artists and writers in the cafés of Paris.

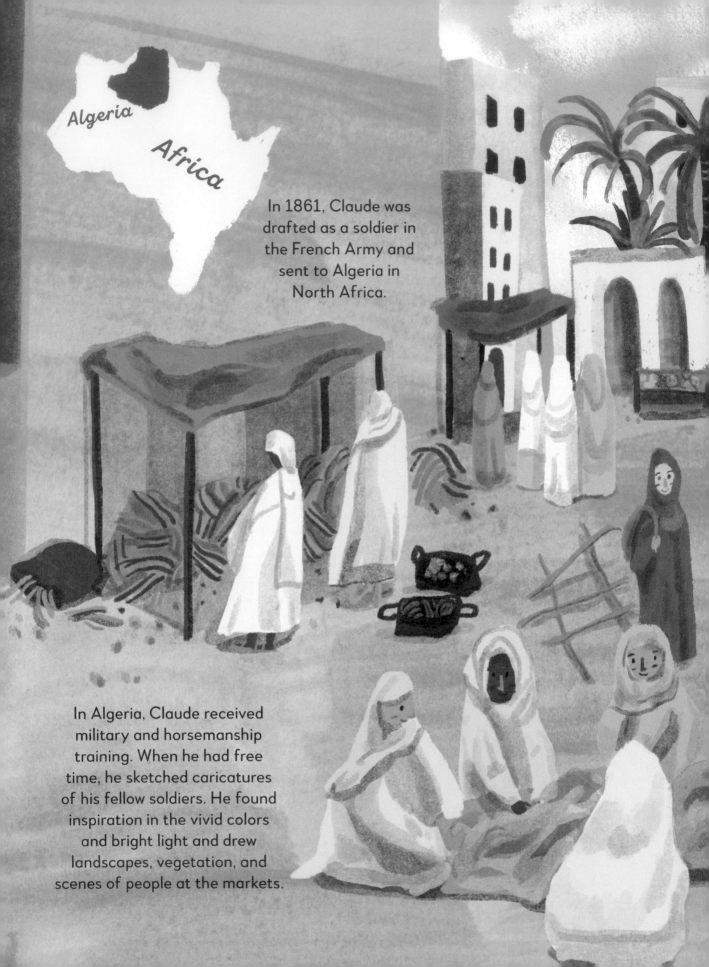

Algeria

Africa

In 1861, Claude was drafted as a soldier in the French Army and sent to Algeria in North Africa.

In Algeria, Claude received military and horsemanship training. When he had free time, he sketched caricatures of his fellow soldiers. He found inspiration in the vivid colors and bright light and drew landscapes, vegetation, and scenes of people at the markets.

But then, Claude fell ill with typhoid fever and was sent back home to France to recover.

In Le Havre, Claude's aunt took care of him, and when he regained his strength, he studied with Dutch landscape artist Johan Jongkind.

His family encouraged Claude to return to Paris, but only if he agreed to take his studies seriously and enroll at Paris's official art school, the famed Ecole des Beaux-Arts. Instead, Claude joined a different studio in Paris, with artist Charles Gleyre, who encouraged students to discover a style of their own.

There, Claude shared a studio with other painters, Jean-Frédéric Bazille, Auguste Renoir, and Alfred Sisley, who were also interested in capturing the dazzling light found in nature. Claude encouraged his friends to paint outside. The young artists went on painting trips around the French countryside. Working hard to convey the sunlight in their artwork, the friends developed a new technique, using quick brushstrokes and daubs of color.

Claude's father had stopped Claude's allowance, leaving him with money problems. None of the other artists had any money either, and, for an entire month, they all lived on one sack of beans.

In 1865, Claude met Camille Doncieux at the studio of a friend. She soon became the model for many of his paintings, and then they fell in love.

Each year in Paris, there was an art show to recognize living artists' works, called the Salon. Thousands of works of art were submitted and most were rejected.

In 1865, two of Claude's paintings of the seaside were accepted into the Salon, and he received praise for his skillful debut. So for the next Salon exhibition, Claude wanted to do something on a grand scale: a giant painting titled *Women in the Garden*. Claude wanted to paint the entire painting outside.

He dug a trench and made a pulley system in his backyard to lower the painting into the ground so he could reach the top. Camille posed several times to represent the four different women in the composition. But he couldn't finish it in time. The next year, Claude had two works accepted into the Salon, including one of Camille in a green dress. It was a triumph!

When Claude finally completed the painting *Women in the Garden* in 1867, the Salon rejected it. The judges were troubled by the artist's heavy brushstrokes and the colorful, sketchy trend that they were also seeing with other young artists. Claude needed money desperately because his artwork wasn't selling, and he was about to become a father.

Try painting a **snowy scene.**
What **colors** *make a scene look* **cold?**

Despite his financial strains, Claude would not stop painting outdoors. Even in the dead of winter, Claude would bundle up in several coats and blankets to paint the purple and blue glow of light on snowy scenes. And in the blazing heat of summer, Claude reproduced the fiery pops of color of the flowers that bloomed by the sea.

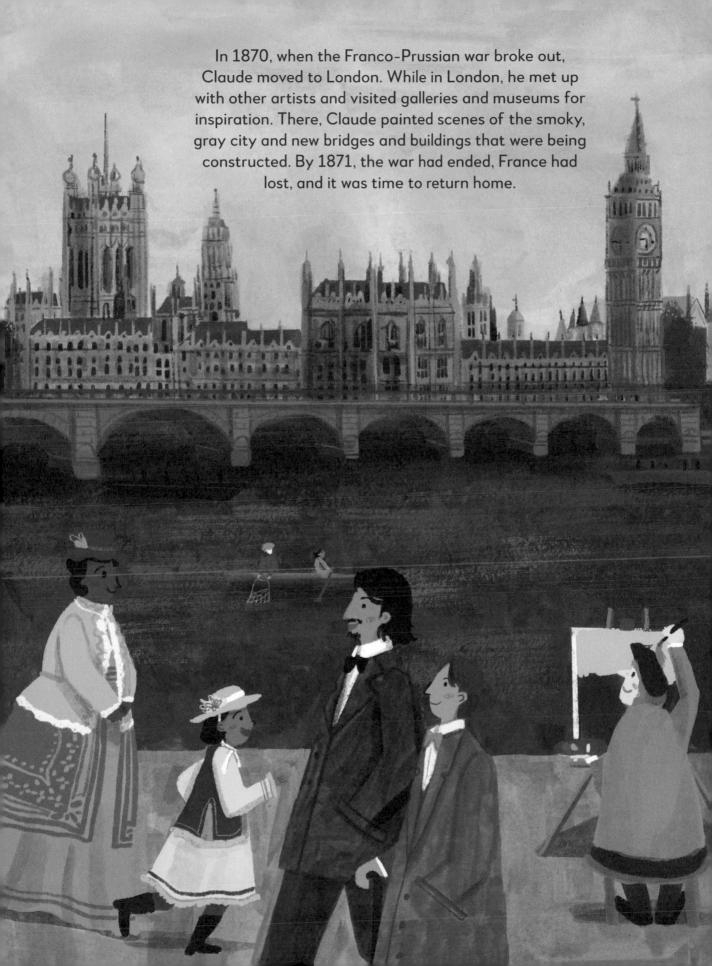

In 1870, when the Franco-Prussian war broke out, Claude moved to London. While in London, he met up with other artists and visited galleries and museums for inspiration. There, Claude painted scenes of the smoky, gray city and new bridges and buildings that were being constructed. By 1871, the war had ended, France had lost, and it was time to return home.

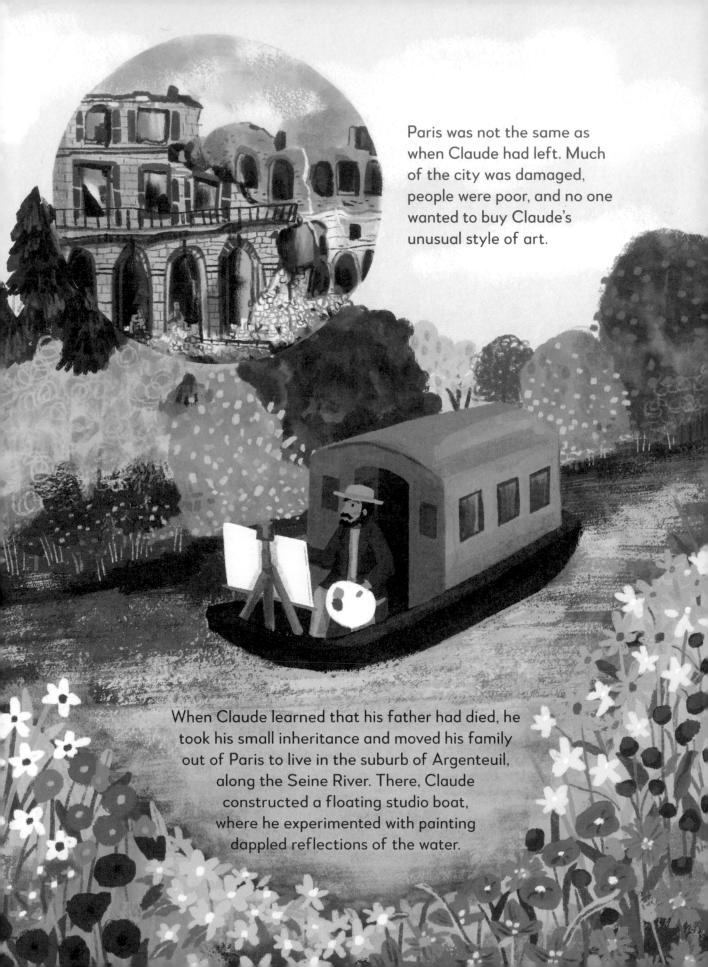

Paris was not the same as when Claude had left. Much of the city was damaged, people were poor, and no one wanted to buy Claude's unusual style of art.

When Claude learned that his father had died, he took his small inheritance and moved his family out of Paris to live in the suburb of Argenteuil, along the Seine River. There, Claude constructed a floating studio boat, where he experimented with painting dappled reflections of the water.

By 1874, Claude and his artist friends grew tired of being rejected by the Salon. They saw that Paris was being rebuilt and becoming a modern city, and they thought it was time for art to change as well. They decided to hold an independent exhibition. The show was not successful, and many people came to laugh at the artwork. One critic called it an "Exhibition of Impressionists," referring to Claude's painting titled *Impression, Sunrise*.

The "Impressionists" name stuck. The artists adopted the tag with pride, and an art movement was born. The group kept holding exhibitions as Impressionist art started to become more accepted.

In 1878, Claude's second son was born. His children were the subject of many of his paintings. But then Camille fell sick, and the family was forced to move in with friends in the village of Vétheuil. Here, Claude continued to paint riverscapes, but also painted Still Lifes of flowers and fruit, because they were easier to sell.

Claude painted a final portrait of Camille while she was ill.
She died in 1879.

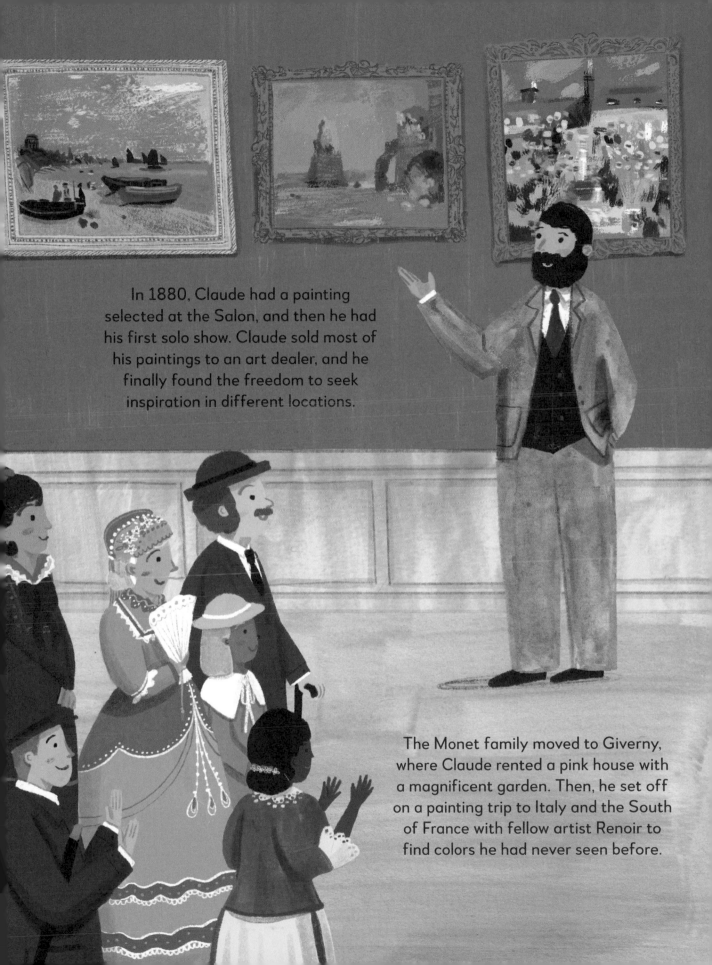

In 1880, Claude had a painting selected at the Salon, and then he had his first solo show. Claude sold most of his paintings to an art dealer, and he finally found the freedom to seek inspiration in different locations.

The Monet family moved to Giverny, where Claude rented a pink house with a magnificent garden. Then, he set off on a painting trip to Italy and the South of France with fellow artist Renoir to find colors he had never seen before.

By the end of the 1880s, Claude had had many art shows across France and around the world. In 1889, he shared the stage with sculptor Auguste Rodin in an art show that was a smashing success.

Imagine decorating your dream house.

What colors would you use?

Then, in 1890, Claude was finally able to buy his pink house and surrounding land in Giverny. Right away, he got to work renovating the house and designing the garden studio. Claude took colors from his own painter's palette to make the green shutters and door, a yellow dining room, and a blue kitchen.

Iris

Claude hired seven gardeners and planted irises,
his favorite flower, in all of the colors of the rainbow.
He planted weeping willows and poplars, bamboo
and blossoming bushes, carnations, azaleas,
larkspurs, tulips, and roses, in every scent and shade.

He created a pond and filled it with water lilies.
The lush garden was soon a majestic place for
children to run free. Other artists would travel
to Claude's garden to paint.

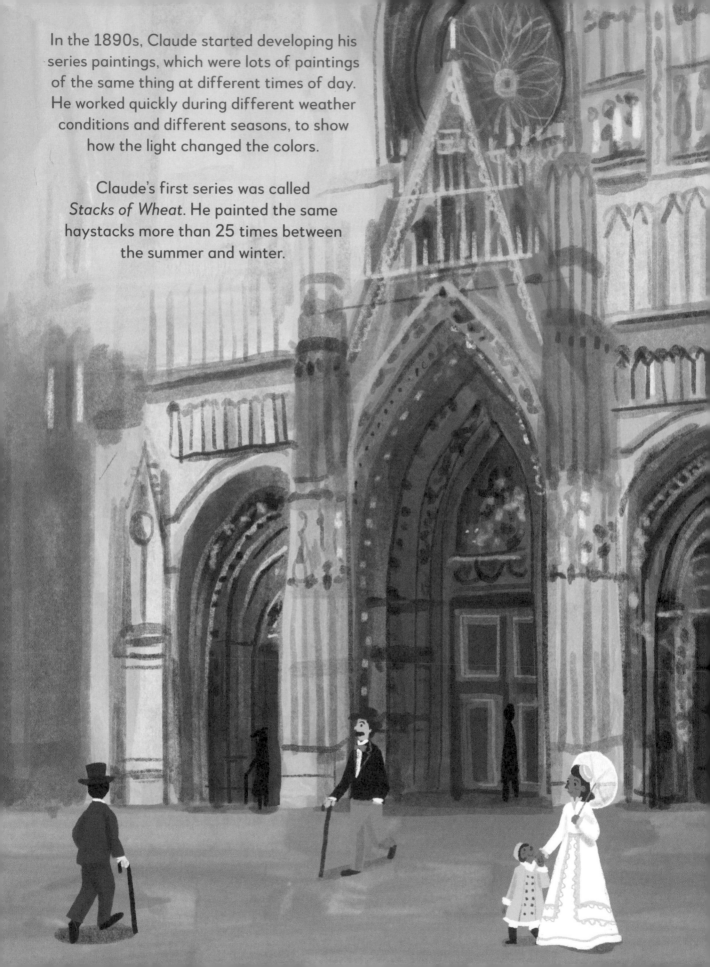

In the 1890s, Claude started developing his series paintings, which were lots of paintings of the same thing at different times of day. He worked quickly during different weather conditions and different seasons, to show how the light changed the colors.

Claude's first series was called *Stacks of Wheat*. He painted the same haystacks more than 25 times between the summer and winter.

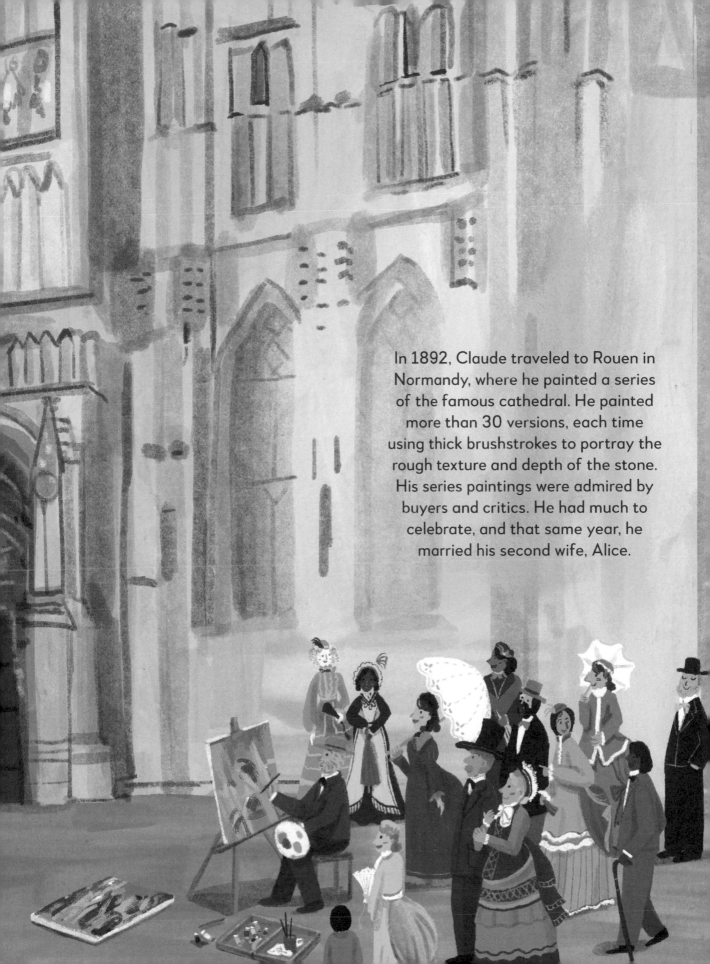

In 1892, Claude traveled to Rouen in Normandy, where he painted a series of the famous cathedral. He painted more than 30 versions, each time using thick brushstrokes to portray the rough texture and depth of the stone. His series paintings were admired by buyers and critics. He had much to celebrate, and that same year, he married his second wife, Alice.

Claude had finally found recognition in the art world and could afford to paint anything he pleased. What pleased him the most was to spend hours in his garden. He kept planning and planting, adding fruit trees and more exotic plants and flowers from around the world. As he sold more paintings, he expanded his gardens and had a Japanese-style bridge built. At this time, he started a series of paintings of his water lilies and his bridge.

He would sit out in the garden under a giant white umbrella surrounded by a collection of colored canvases that had been started at different times of day. One by one, he would add to the paintings, a dab of pink next to a stroke of purple, each mark placed just so.

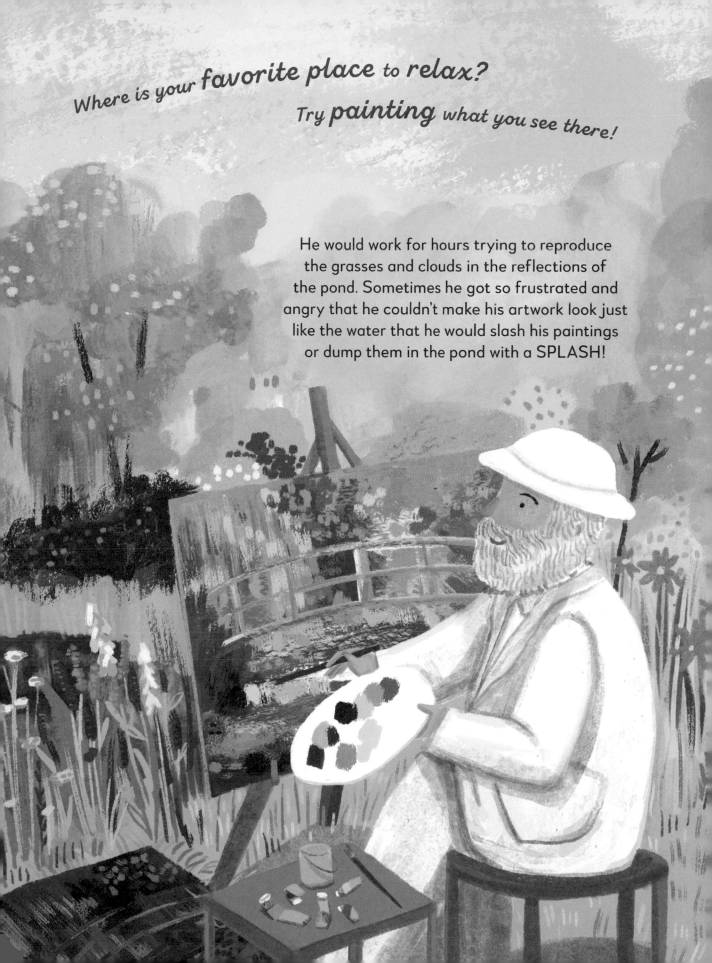

Where is your **favorite place** to **relax?**

Try **painting** what you see there!

He would work for hours trying to reproduce the grasses and clouds in the reflections of the pond. Sometimes he got so frustrated and angry that he couldn't make his artwork look just like the water that he would slash his paintings or dump them in the pond with a SPLASH!

In 1900, Claude had an eye accident and had to stop working for a short time. Claude's eye problems were only beginning, but in the early 1900s, he kept traveling and painting. First, he visited London, where he painted a series of the Houses of Parliament. For over four years, he painted fog, rain, mist, and soft light.

Choose a building you find interesting. Try painting it at different times of day.

While he was in London, Claude had a wildly successful show in the United States. His London series was also a hit, so he bought a car and drove his family to Spain for a much-needed vacation.

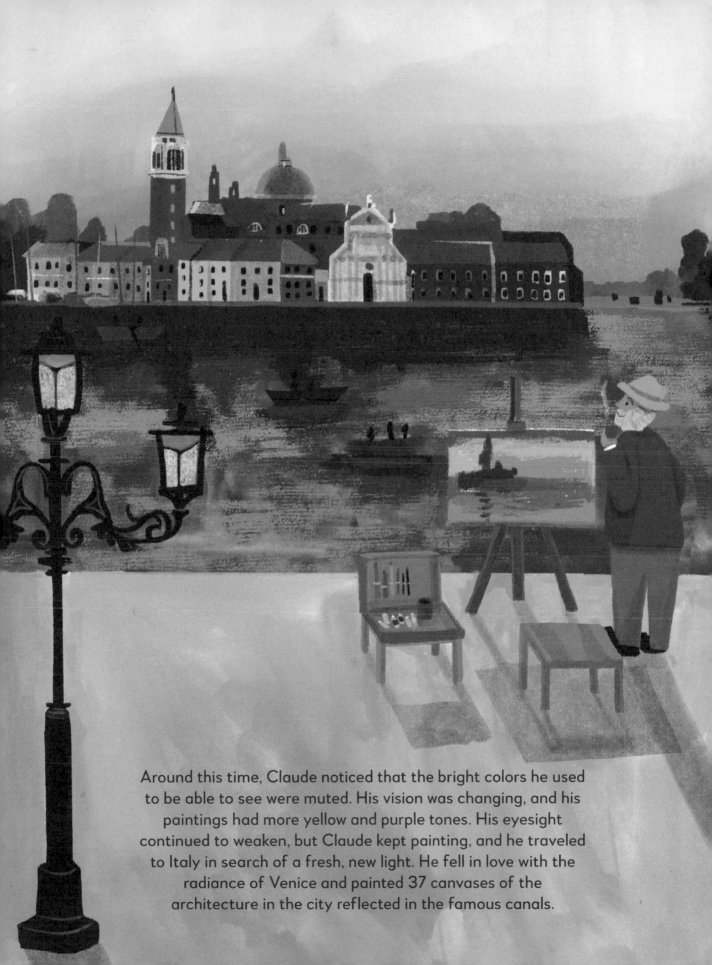

Around this time, Claude noticed that the bright colors he used
to be able to see were muted. His vision was changing, and his
paintings had more yellow and purple tones. His eyesight
continued to weaken, but Claude kept painting, and he traveled
to Italy in search of a fresh, new light. He fell in love with the
radiance of Venice and painted 37 canvases of the
architecture in the city reflected in the famous canals.

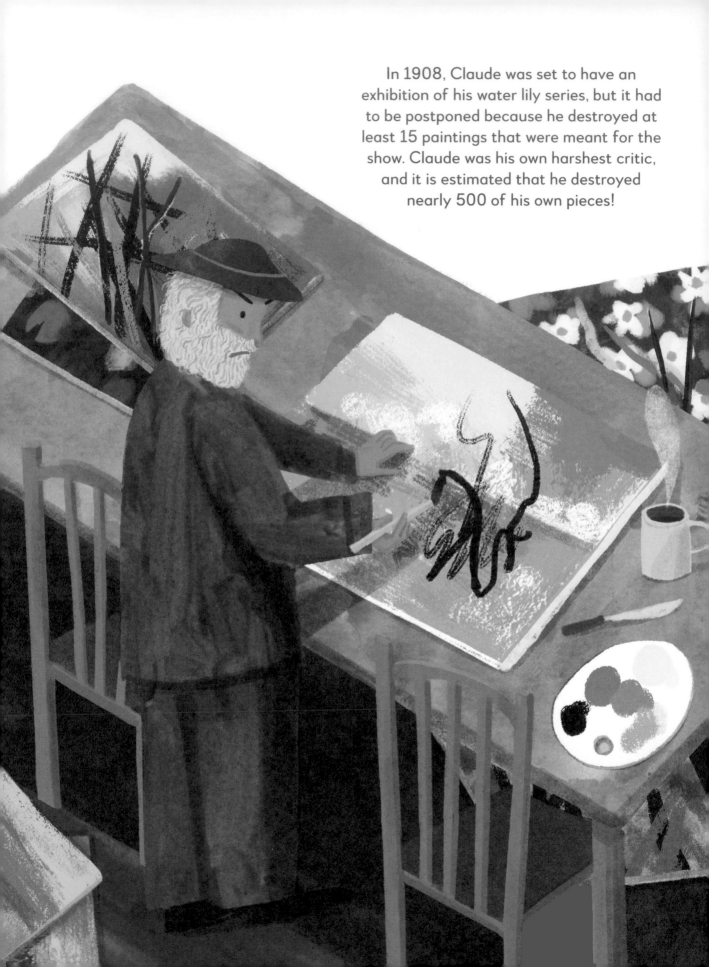

In 1908, Claude was set to have an exhibition of his water lily series, but it had to be postponed because he destroyed at least 15 paintings that were meant for the show. Claude was his own harshest critic, and it is estimated that he destroyed nearly 500 of his own pieces!

Do you have a favorite flower?
Try painting or drawing it!

In 1909, Claude finally exhibited his 48 paintings from the water lily series to great fanfare. But then his wife grew sick and died, and then his son died, too. Claude was very sad but he found comfort by tending to his flowers, and gradually his spirits began to lift.

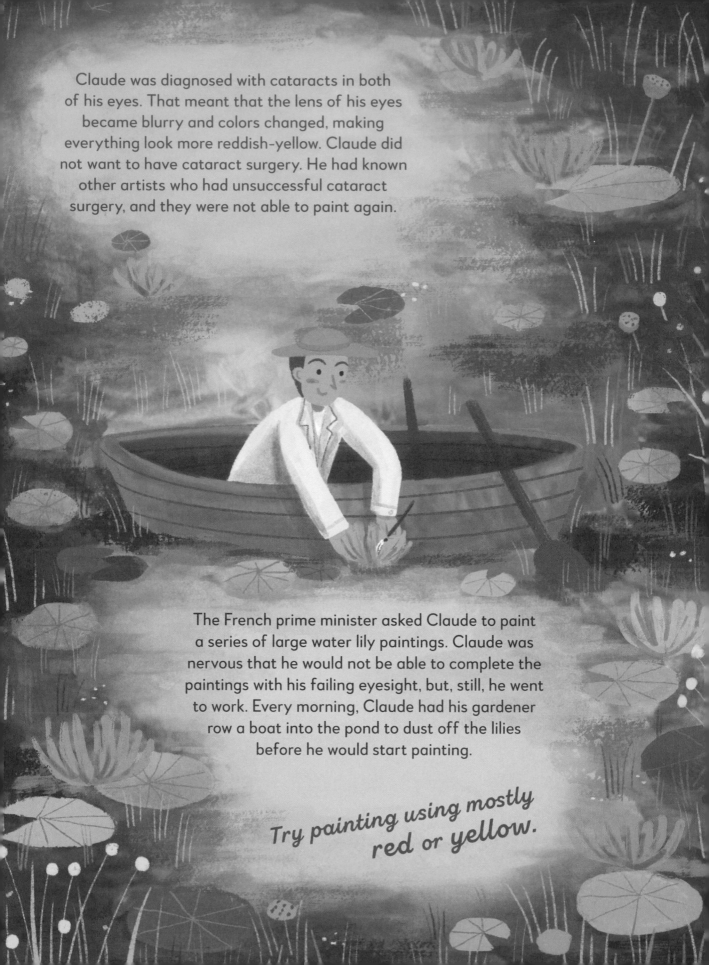

Claude was diagnosed with cataracts in both of his eyes. That meant that the lens of his eyes became blurry and colors changed, making everything look more reddish-yellow. Claude did not want to have cataract surgery. He had known other artists who had unsuccessful cataract surgery, and they were not able to paint again.

The French prime minister asked Claude to paint a series of large water lily paintings. Claude was nervous that he would not be able to complete the paintings with his failing eyesight, but, still, he went to work. Every morning, Claude had his gardener row a boat into the pond to dust off the lilies before he would start painting.

Try painting using mostly red or yellow.

By 1918, Claude had completed eight large water lily paintings. Now, he could no longer see violets and blues, so he rarely painted with these colors. But finally, in 1923, Claude agreed to have cataract surgery. It was a success! He was given special glasses, and he could see violets and blues again. These colors returned to his paintings.

"My garden is my most beautiful masterpiece."

—Claude Monet

Claude kept painting new works and enjoying
his beautiful home and gardens. He spent
the last ten years of his life painting his
large *Water Lilies* paintings for France.

In 1926, Claude died in Giverny at the age of 86.

Claude's artwork and his garden lived on.
He had become one of France's most
important and famous artists. In 1927,
at the Musée de l'Orangerie in Paris,
eight paintings from his *Water Lilies* series
were installed. The enormous panels were
exhibited according to Claude's wishes in
an immersive oval display, representing
the cycle of light throughout the day.

Today, more than 500,000 visitors
tour his garden at Giverny each year.

Timeline of key artworks

Throughout his long career from the mid-19th century to the early 20th century, Claude Monet created more than 2,500 paintings, drawings, and pastels. Here are a few of his key works, all in the collection of The Metropolitan Museum of Art.

"I perhaps owe having become a painter to flowers."

–Claude Monet

1867 *Garden at Sainte-Adresse*
Oil on canvas

1869 *La Grenouillere*
Oil on canvas

1873 *Camille Monet on a Garden Bench*
Oil on canvas

1878 *Parc Monceau*
Oil on canvas

1880 *Sunflowers*
Oil on canvas

1886 *Manneporte near Etretat*
Oil on canvas

Timeline continued:

1891 Haystacks (Effect
of Snow and Sun)
Oil on canvas

1894
Rouen Cathedral:
The Portal (Sunlight)
Oil on canvas

1897 Morning on the
Seine near Giverny
Oil on canvas

*"Color is my day-long obsession,
joy and torment."*
–Claude Monet

1899 *Bridge over a Pond of Water Lilies*
Oil on canvas

1903-4
The Houses of Parliament (Effect of Fog.)
Oil on canvas

1919 *Water Lilies*
Oil on canvas

Make a Japanese Bridge Painting

Using bright, bold daubs of color, Claude Monet captured the reflection of his water lilies on the water.

Try to recreate Claude Monet's *Bridge over a Pond of Water Lilies* by using short brushstrokes and daubs of different colors. Place the colors next to each other so that they mix together to create a new color when you stand back. This manner of painting is called "broken color," and it is a technique that the Impressionist painters used to paint the effects of light.

Bridge over a Pond of Water Lilies, 1899

"I would like to paint the way a bird sings."

–Claude Monet

Create your own version.

Don't worry if you can't find a real bridge to paint—paint from your imagination, or use Claude Monet's bridge painting or the picture opposite as a reference. Start by sketching the bridge and then fill in the entire painting with daubs of colors to create the details. Add different types of lines to show grass, leaves, petals, and lily pads.

For a greater challenge, take your supplies and paint *en plein air*—outside!

Haystack Object Series

For a year (1890–1891), Claude Monet created 30 paintings focusing on the haystacks in a field near his house. He painted several series of paintings so he could experiment with capturing light.

Try painting a **tree** at **different times** of day.

Claude Monet explained to an art critic about his efforts, "I am working very hard, struggling with a series of different effects, but at this season the sun sets so fast I cannot follow it ... The more I continue, the more I see that a great deal of work is necessary in order to succeed in rendering what I seek."

Find an object outside that is easy to paint over and over again. Did you find a tree? A house? A fire hydrant? A stop sign? What will you paint?

Try to capture the light reflecting off the object at different times of the day and in different weather conditions. What do you notice about the changing light and colors?

Try your own series painting!

Haystacks (Effect of Snow and Sun) 1891

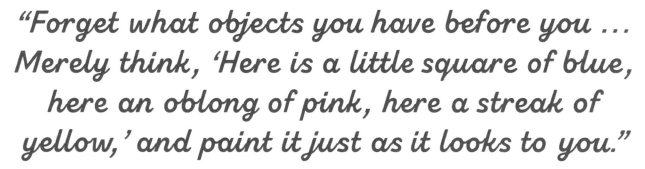

"*Forget what objects you have before you ... Merely think, 'Here is a little square of blue, here an oblong of pink, here a streak of yellow,' and paint it just as it looks to you.*"

–Claude Monet

Glossary

Caricatures
A drawing of a person where certain features of its subject are exaggerated for comic effect.

Critic
A person who judges the merits of a work of art.

En plein air (in the open air)
A manner of painting outdoors that became a central feature of French Impressionism.

Gallery
A building or room that features works of art for show or sale.

Impressionists
A group of artists in the late 19th and early 20th centuries who used broken, unblended brushstrokes and paid special attention to light and its effect on subjects in their paintings. They were interested in painting scenes from modern life.

Landscape
A picture that represents an area of the countryside.

Modern Art
A style and period of art between the late 19th and the late 20th centuries that rejected traditional techniques of the past in the spirit of experimentation.

Muse
A person who serves as an artist's inspiration.

Portrait
An image of a person, especially one of the head and shoulders.

Salon
An annual exhibition of the work of living artists held by the Ecole des Beaux-Arts (School of Fine Arts) in Paris.

Still Life
A painting or drawing of an arrangement of objects, like flowers in a vase or fruit in a bowl.

Studio
A room where an artist works.

Amy Guglielmo

Amy Guglielmo is an author, artist, arts educator, and arts advocate. She has written many books for children, including *Cezanne's Parrot* and *Just Being Dali: The Story of Artist Salvador Dali*. Amy has co-authored the picture books *Pocket Full of Colors: The Magical World of Mary Blair*, winner of the Christopher Award; *How to Build a Hug: Temple Grandin and Her Amazing Squeeze Machine*; and the Touch the Art series of novelty board books featuring famous works of art with tactile additions. She lives on Lake Champlain with her husband.

Ginnie Hsu

Ginnie Hsu is a Visual Storyteller living in Upstate New York. Her work is often inspired by everyday life, nature, and well-being. She believes good stories incorporate an awareness of humans and society, observation of problems, constant learning, and a desire to research and empathise. She loves exploring new ways to tell stories and hopes to contribute work that effects meaningful change in the world. When she's not in her studio, she loves gardening and spending time in nature with her dogs.

Project Editor Rosie Peet
Project Art Editor Chris Gould
Designer Clare Baggaley
Picture Researchers Martin Copeland,
Taiyaba Khatoon, and Aditya Katyal
Production Editor Siu Yin Chan
Production Controller Louise Minihane
Senior Acquisitions Editor Katy Flint
Managing Art Editor Vicky Short
Publishing Director Mark Searle

First American Edition, 2022
Published in the United States by DK Publishing
1745 Broadway, 20th Floor, New York NY 10019

Page design copyright © 2022 Dorling Kindersley Limited
DK, a Division of Penguin Random House LLC
23 24 25 26 10 9 8 7 6 5 4 3 2
004–327549–May/2022

The Metropolitan
Museum of Art
New York

©The Metropolitan Museum of Art

All rights reserved.
Without limiting the rights under the copyright reserved above, no part of this
publication may be reproduced, stored in or introduced into a retrieval system,
or transmitted, in any form, or by any means (electronic, mechanical,
photocopying, recording, or otherwise), without the prior written permission
of the copyright owner.
Published in Great Britain by Dorling Kindersley Limited

A catalog record for this book
is available from the Library of Congress.
ISBN 978-0-7440-5470-5

DK books are available at special discounts when purchased
in bulk for sales promotions, premiums, fund-raising, or educational use.
For details, contact: DK Publishing Special Markets,
1745 Broadway, 20th Floor, New York NY 10019
SpecialSales@dk.com

Printed and bound in China

Acknowledgments
DK would like to thank Laura Corey, Susan Stein,
Lisa Silverman Meyers, and Morgan Pearce at The Met;
Hilary Becker; Clare Baggaley; Amy Guglielmo and Ginnie Hsu;
and Jennette ElNaggar for proofreading. The author would like
to thank the lovely Laura Clary.

For the curious

www.dk.com
www.metmuseum.org

This book was made with Forest
Stewardship Council™ certified
paper – one small step in DK's
commitment to a sustainable future.
For more information go to
www.dk.com/our-green-pledge

Picture credits

The publisher would like to thank the following for their kind permission to reproduce their photographs:

(Key: a-above; b-below/bottom; c-center; f-far; l-left; r-right; t-top)

40 © The Metropolitan Museum of Art: H. O. Havemeyer Collection, Bequest of Mrs. H. O. Havemeyer, 1929 (crb); Purchase, special contributions and funds given or bequeathed by friends of the Museum, 1967 (cl). **40-41 Shutterstock.com:** Quirky Mundo. **41 © The Metropolitan Museum of Art:** Bequest of Lillie P. Bliss, 1931 (crb); The Walter H. and Leonore Annenberg Collection, Gift of Walter H. and Leonore Annenberg, 2002, Bequest of Walter H. Annenberg, 2002 (tl); The Mr. and Mrs. Henry Ittleson Jr. Purchase Fund, 1959 (tr); H. O. Havemeyer Collection, Bequest of Mrs. H. O. Havemeyer, 1929 (clb). **42-43 Shutterstock.com:** Quirky Mundo. **42 © The Metropolitan Museum of Art:** Bequest of Julia W. Emmons, 1956 (crb); Theodore M. Davis Collection, Bequest of Theodore M. Davis, 1915 (cl); H. O. Havemeyer Collection, Bequest of Mrs. H. O. Havemeyer, 1929 (tc). **43 © The Metropolitan Museum of Art:** Bequest of Julia W. Emmons, 1956 (tr); H. O. Havemeyer Collection, Bequest of Mrs. H. O. Havemeyer, 1929 (tl); The Walter H. and Leonore Annenberg Collection, Gift of Walter H. and Leonore Annenberg, 1998, Bequest of Walter H. Annenberg, 2002 (cb). **44 © The Metropolitan Museum of Art:** H. O. Havemeyer Collection, Bequest of Mrs. H. O. Havemeyer, 1929 (cb). **45 123RF.com:** SOMPOB TAPAOPONG (clb). **46 Dreamstime.com:** Gavril Bernad (cl). **47 © The Metropolitan Museum of Art:** H. O. Havemeyer Collection, Bequest of Mrs. H. O. Havemeyer, 1929 (c)

All other images © Dorling Kindersley
For further information see: www.dkimages.com